WELL WORTH WAITING FOR

Well Worth Waiting For

Frank W Payne

Matador
9 Priory Business Park,
Wistow Road, Kibworth Beauchamp,
Leicestershire. LE8 0RX
Tel: 0116 279 2299
Email: books@troubador.co.uk
Web: www.troubador.co.uk/matador
Twitter: @matadorbooks

ISBN 978 1800463 882

British Library Cataloguing in Publication Data.
A catalogue record for this book is available from the British Library.

Printed and bound in Great Britain by 4edge Limited
Typeset in 12pt Minion Pro by Troubador Publishing Ltd, Leicester, UK

Matador is an imprint of Troubador Publishing Ltd

ONE

Driving through the evening motorway madness. Still wrestling with embarrassed anger. Never once believing I would ever discover feet I hated more than my own. The threat of losing the agency's largest account still ringing in my ears, of one thing I was certain. Graham, my partner, was a dead man. As I entered the unlit stairwell of my small Chelmsford office, I failed to notice them. Them being his feet. Encased in rundown shoes. Soles full of holes. Protruding out of the darkness. I tripped over them. Crashed to the floor. Found myself lying on the inert figure of Graham, my partner. Almost cheek to cheek, unconscious, unwashed, wreathed in the perfume of drunken alcoholism. Liberally laced with incontinence.

Graham, alcoholic by choice, my partner by default. Advertising genius when sober; unreliable, uncontrollable to the point of being unreasonable when not. Given a full month to produce a new product launch advertising campaign introducing the first ever UK portable dictating machine. It had been a huge success when first launched in America and was now on its way to these isles. The American company's chief executive officer had insisted the USA promotion campaign be used here in Great Britain, virtually in its entirety. I tried very hard to explain. No, not the identical campaign. It clearly needed anglicising, treating as an innovative UK new product, fully supported by the UK management team. Eventually, a compromise was reached. It was translatable, giving Graham a free hand in product advertising and graphic design. This was agreed, provided the American CEO attended the UK launch presentation campaign in Leamington Spa. It would be either his thumbs up, or down. If the latter, the USA campaign it would be. Though it wasn't said at the time, lose the battle, lose the account too. It was our biggest. A massive responsibility on Graham's shoulders. But the unreliable bastard hadn't been seen for days.

Graham, my partner, whom I first met eighteen months previously. Whose company was financially knackered, whose other director walked away taking the one company car with him. Leaving just one active recruitment account, now Graham's only client. I had no idea then he was a fully paid-up member of Alcoholics Anonymous. But, he had something I wanted. A small office-come-studio in Chelmsford. He gave me the office. I paid the rent; in exchange, I made him my partner verbally, which I very soon came to regret. Now, more so than ever. For some time, he lived between his girlfriend's house and our small office junk room. Whenever drunk. Now more often than not. Graham, my partner, I paid him nothing, he was worth even less.

Best I spoke to him early morning. I did, before the pubs opened, giving him an in-depth briefing on the portable hand-held dictation machine. He made copious notes. Accompanied me on three client visits to Leamington Spa and questioned all concerned with the sales and marketing of the product. Drank Coke when we lunched with them. Best of all, the first campaign roughs were most impressive, Graham, my partner, at his level best. I was excited with everything to date. And told him so.

It was the final week before the Leamington Spa trade/national press advertising, marketing and public relations campaign presentation. I loved everything Graham had produced. Now they needed finishing, to the highest possible standard. He knew it. I knew it. He promised. I promised. He would receive payment for what he had done. He went home happy. I went home happy. Then panic. I didn't see him again. Until there he was. Unconscious in the darkened stairwell. Unkempt. Dirty. Smelly. After the day I'd had, I wanted to kill him. How I kept my hands off him I will never know.

Until now, nobody knew where he was. Only that he was desperately needed. We hunted but to no avail.

The bastard was nowhere to be seen. Because of the launch timing and the fact the American CEO was already here, I had to ring Leamington. In business, you learned to lie competently, exceptionally well when the chips were down. Mine was an Oscar-winning performance, on the telephone, explaining Graham (no longer my partner) had gone down with Asian flu. Now confined to (his partner's) bed and slowly recovering. Whatever condition his health was in, he promised he would finish the job and present it on the Thursday of next week. I was so believable, the USA chief executive officer extended his UK visit.

I stayed there in the dimly lit stairwell, trying desperately to suppress the overwhelming desire to break both his ankles. Instead I took a large piece of white board and a marker. I wrote "I want the finished ads and artwork on my desk on Wednesday morning. I will make the presentation. Alone." He must have burnt the midnight oil. Everything was finished to an impeccable standard. Graham at his very best.

I made the presentation alone. The whole campaign was accepted. Later I thanked Graham, then asked him to leave. He did and I never did see or hear from him again. Not long after, the client appointed his previous agency. There were now two of us handling the same business. It was not big enough. Their share was growing, ours noticeably shrinking. Soon after, the Yanks called the UK MD back Stateside. I knew then our time together was over. I was called to Leamington and lunched by the new marketing manager. The food, as ever, was good. The news that our services were no longer needed wasn't.

Two

Following an acrimonious departure from the Royal Air Force, then losing an excellent career opportunity after just one month through someone convinced he was a water walker, you might just say depression was a frequent, if unwelcome visitor. Here I was. Out of the RAF. Out of a job. Decidedly out of money. Definitely avoiding anything Air Force. Perhaps it was to keep the pint and cigarettes company, I bought the *Royal Air Force Flying Review* with money borrowed from my mother. That's how bad it was. I inattentively thumbed through it starting at the rear, where all the classified jobs were published along with the *Flying Review*'s very own.

I wondered, could it be I'd find a towed target operator vacancy? The last job I did in the RAF, and enormously enjoyed. But I was only joshing. I had far greater chance of finding a funeral director's vacancy in the *Beano*. But, there it was. On the very next page. Small but eye-catching. 'Young man wanted to train as advertising salesman'. Before I'd digested the full content, I was heading for the nearest phone. Within minutes I had an appointment with Mr Matthews, Group Classified Advertising Manager. I was twenty years old. What's more, I'd never sold a single thing in my life. But just fifteen minutes after sitting in front of Matty, as he loved to be called, I was on the Business Publications payroll. I never had an easier job interview in my life.

Matty's was a voice only he could love. It was a high-pitched, sing-song falsetto. When he became excited, his words assaulted each other. This happened often, for he never stopped reciting how successful his business life had been. For all of the time he was talking, he lit and re-lit his pipe. It smelt like raw sewage, laced with creosote. It was putrid. Have you ever sat through thirty minutes of bullshit, inhaling the aforementioned stench? Bet you haven't. My endeavours deserved to be rewarded with employment. They were. I became a new under-training advertising salesman the following Monday. I was now one of a group of Business Publications' representatives, could you believe, on the *Royal Air Force Flying Review*. If the advertisement or Matty had mentioned the title – there were six trade magazines in the group – I would never have joined. I was gobsmacked. So here I was. Standing on Kidbrooke railway station in what is now known as south east London, waiting along with dozens of fellow passengers as the Charing Cross train arrived.

They crouched, collectively, fists raised, battle ready. Crowding the area where the third-class carriages would grind to a jerky halt. Mostly men, few women. They were further away. Standing where they hoped the 'Ladies Only' carriages would halt, introduced in respect of women travellers. I say bring them back. Remove girls' embarrassment at the groping hands of untold travelling male 'dirty buggers'. Rid British Rail of these dirty old sods. Once and for all. The train stopped. I was virtually lifted off my feet and deposited in the middle of a sea of pushing, shoving, elbowing humanity. No chance of a seat. It didn't matter. Then, third-class carriage seats were wooden.

I arrived at our scruffy, temporary Carmelite Street offices just before nine o'clock. Only Matty was present. He welcomed me and showed me to my small, scruffy desk. On it were files and back issues of the *Royal Air Force Flying Review* together with the previous salesman's client call reports. Now I was no salesman, but within minutes I suspected many of them were fictitious. Pure bullshit. They were exactly what I would have wanted to read. But only if I had been his boss. By the time the other salesmen had arrived, I had read enough. I could follow my predecessor, hoodwink Matty for as long as it took him to realise the truth, be unemployed again within six months. Or, looking again at the advertising revenue he had sold, work hard, double, treble, quadruple it and leave at my convenience. That was my decision. But, never having previously sold for a living, could I do it? I shook the hand of the other five occupants. Listened to Matty's call for action. Watched and listened to each salesman setting up appointments before leaving for his day's/week's pre-arranged calls. Or so I, and of course Matty, believed.

I spent my first week familiarising myself with the *Flying Review*. Its past year's performance. Those areas of commerce, industry, finance and insurance with the greatest consumption of young demobees leaving the services. The other salesmen left the office. All within half an hour of each other. Strange, or so I thought. For the rest of the week I had the phone stuck to my ear. Result. Enough appointments to fill my first month.

It was five-thirty on Friday. Home-going time. My colleagues were going to the pub. I willingly agreed when asked. It was a warning couched in a friendly gesture. Was I some sort of nut? A head case? Was I keen to gain fat Matty's favours? Was I one of those rare creatures, a workaholic? By now I was getting up-tight. And it showed. What followed was given on trust, never to reach Matty's ears. I promised. If ever it did it wouldn't be through me, I'd swear on a stack of Bibles if that's what they wanted. This is what I learned. A routine practised by Matty's disciples. Without his knowledge of course.

First and foremost, each knew the approximate monthly financial advertising turnover Matty would accept. Once reached, the selling brakes were applied. You earned salary only. Commission was not paid. So why keep grafting once you had achieved what Matty wanted? I asked why they left at around the same time each day. Their reply was a great surprise. They made their way to the old Bow Street Court. These were the days when prostitution, though criminal, was openly practised on the streets of London. Mainly the West End. It was both immoral and illegal so at irregular intervals each sex worker was arrested. They appeared during the Court's morning sessions. Once in the dock, they were asked their name, age and address. Then a charge of living on immoral earnings was quickly read out. Asked how they pleaded, they replied guilty. The Magistrate then fined them two pounds, fifty shillings each. It was continuously demoralised feminine immorality. The punishment never varied. Once recorded, the Judge called for the next to appear. It was as quick as that. A conveyor belt of sex for sale, with the whole of Matty's sales force in attendance. Taking details of the best-looking ladies of the night. Then onto the Kardomah Coffee House. Sustenance. After which, their business of the day began.

They watched closely for my reaction to what I had been told. I explained that this was my first job, having recently completed National Service. It was my intention to work hard and build the advertising revenue of *Flying Review* to Matty's satisfaction. Look for promotion within the group. If not found, move on.

It didn't suit me to immediately fall in with their daily routine. Perhaps now and again. Then gave my word I'd tell no one of what they did. I asked what happened to my *Flying Review* predecessor. They laughed out loud. He lasted just over four months. Not only was he paid by Business Publications; for three days a week he was also a barman in a Soho pub. Working for *Flying Review*, most of his sales reports were fictitious, his duplicate pub salary an adequate return for his cheek.

And so it began. My first full-time senior employment. Nothing spectacular. Under a boss who I believed was 'trainable'. My plan of action from day one; select an eclectic bunch of potential clients, from those readily available. Ignore the accompanying file reports. Most were fiction. Not fact. Ring for appointments. Next week where possible. Within the month if not. Write to confirm. Tell them of your recent background. Two years in the RAF. Amongst a very large body of young men and women, the very audience their classified advertisements were targeted to reach. I made certain Matty was kept aware of my early progress. Which, though I say it myself, was impressive in appointments logged, calls made, business written. Watched and warned by the rest of Matty's sales team; 'Don't let on about what we do.' What kind of pillock did they take me for?

Eventually we moved from Carmelite Street to our new, comprehensive modern office block opposite Waterloo Station. Luxury compared to our previous accommodation. All of our goods and chattels were deposited in our new reception. We were then expected to hump them into our open-plan, half-partitioned new offices. Disadvantage. Nowhere to hide when returning from a forbidden client liquid lunch. But then, I'd already spotted one distinct advantage. An attractive young brunette with large, friendly 'whammers'. Already I was on a mission to discover just how friendly, for my book of social graces said, "Whenever confronted by what you deem friendly, offer your hand." When the opportunity presented itself, I did. Three years later, she became my wife.

I was both happy and successful selling recruitment advertising on *Flying Review*. I stuck to my original game plan. Salesmen on other group publications came and went. I stayed, the job now honed to my exact specification. It suited me admirably. I was Matty's favourite and would be for as long as I remained. At the same time, subtle hints of complacency appeared on my career horizon with increasing frequency. Were they warning me it was time to seek something new? Would I find it in *Advertisers Weekly*? Another Group Publication whose classifieds I decided to start looking at. And there it was. Small, but to me most meaningful. It was a box number, which surprised me. Wanted was an enthusiastic, young space salesman for a yet-to-be-launched office equipment trade magazine. Successful, hardworking, innovative. Seeking a salary commensurate with an exciting career.

It was as if I had written the advertisement myself. For myself. That evening I sat and wrote my reply. I pulled no punches. Phrases like "I have sold both classified and display advertising to the best of my ability. And the delight of my bosses. I've had my advertising manager looking over his shoulder for months. Appoint me if you want a launch to be proud of. If not, like me you will have to look elsewhere." Shoot from the hip. Display an air of confidence. Tell it like it is. Although he wouldn't like me leaving, Matty I'm certain would provide me with an excellent reference. Almost to the extent of allowing me to write it myself. That's how strong our relationship had grown. However, the box number had thrown me. After eighteen months, I thought I knew every recruitment advertisement my company had ever written. That is, except this one. Two weeks had passed without sign of a reply. It was a well-written advertisement so no doubt the replies received were many. Impatiently I continued to wait for the reply I never, ever received.

Matty stopped me on my way out to the day's first calls. "What have you been up to Frank? The managing director wants to see you at four-thirty today."

Being the saucy sod I am, quick as a flash I replied, "He's probably going to offer me your job, Matty."

I had three appointments that day. All were heads of Human Resources. All were women. All were liked by me. All were good for business. Each in turn asked if there was something on my mind. When I told them of my pending MD afternoon meeting, I was wished the best of luck.

I reported to Sally, the managing director's PA. It was four-twenty. Sally knew why I was there but when asked she wouldn't let on. Said nowt. Only that I'd know soon enough. At exactly four-thirty the door slowly opened. There stood the great man, JH (as he liked to be known). He ushered me into his office. Sat me down. Then climbed upon the corner of his desk, sat facing me. We sat like this for what seemed, for me, a nervous eternity. Then he reached behind him and produced an envelope. "Seen this before young Payne?" he said. Before I could answer he continued, "You should have. You wrote it." The penny dropped. At the same time I recognised the envelope. I was gobsmacked. Mouth open. Face beetroot red. I know I was awaiting a reply to my recent job application, but not from my own managing director. "So you're keen to leave us young Payne," he said.

Having been rumbled, I decided to go for broke. "No Sir," I said. "But I now know I am better than the classified job I've been doing for the past two years."

JH smiled. "I've checked the details in your application with Matty. He agrees. But not every young man writes and tells his managing director just how good he thinks he is."

It was here I went for broke. "Give me the chance Sir and I'll prove it."

His reply I could hardly believe. "Now I've met you and taking into account Matty's high opinion of you, go upstairs and introduce yourself to Arthur Norris. Tell him you are his new representative. JH said so."

I was ecstatic. "Thank you JH," I said. Then added cheekily, "You've made the right decision."

He smiled as he replied, "I'll be the judge of that."

THREE

Arthur Norris wasn't in his office and was not expected to return that evening. I explained who I was and why I was there to Ann, his secretary. I told her JH had appointed me that afternoon. She made me feel most welcome and showed me to my desk in the outer office. I knew Norris by sight but had never spoken to him. Ann said he was the most hard-working boss she had ever worked for; he had joined Business Publications four months previously solely to launch *Office Equipment News*. I asked Ann did she think he and I would get on? Work well together?

"Frank," she said, putting on her coat, "you will if you do what he wants. Eat, sleep and breathe the new magazine. Work twelve hours each day. Do not fail to meet the monthly advertising sales targets he sets you. Goodnight." With that she was gone.

All weekend those six words haunted me. "If you do what he wants." Then again I thought, *What the hell will happen if he doesn't like what I want?*

It was Monday. As I entered our new offices at 8.50am I was soon to find out. As expected, my new boss was already seated at his desk. I was about to knock. He beat me to it. Spun in his chair, bid me enter and apologised for being absent on Friday. Made a big issue of telling me why. It was his last call of the day. Staring intently at me, the questioning began. How well did I know the office equipment market? How long had I been selling display advertising? On which publication? Question after question. I was still standing just inside the door. Never a welcome. A friendly 'good morning'. A warm handshake. I gathered from his attitude he had expected to appoint his own junior salesman. Not JH. That he hadn't annoyed him, left him feeling JH did not trust his judgement. His anger further increased when told JH had also written and placed the advertisement himself, never telling him the vacancy was no more. JH didn't know it at the time but by doing so, what had worried me all weekend had already started. Six months later I was seeking different employment.

You will recall, earlier my attention was drawn to a rather well-endowed brunette. In the six months I tolerated the animosity of Arthur Norris, we became an item. On March 29th 2020 we celebrated our sixty-second wedding anniversary. Her name was Patricia Anne Medlock. And yes. She was an Essex girl. This I didn't know when first we met. I very soon found out. I had been seconded to shift furniture from Carmelite Street to the new Waterloo offices. It was a cold, wet, miserable day. I was wearing my recently purchased oversized, overlong black overcoat, sold to me by a sharp, sweet-talking, Jewish Sunday market Petticoat Lane shop owner. He convinced me 'baggy' big was this year's incoming male fashion, while gathering and holding the spare material behind my back. Then dropping the price by three pounds. That was the clincher. When Pat first saw me in it, standing beside piles of office furniture, she convinced herself I was a removal man. I winked. She laughed out loud. Here was a challenge. One I accepted. Especially as I had an angry, very painful large boil at the back of my neck. Every step in my bell-tent of a suspect black overcoat, carrying heavy office furniture up two flights of stairs, was purgatory. Whether it was the coat or the way I was walking, trying to relieve the pain, I was determined to find out. I did. Two years later she became Mrs Payne.

It transpired our offices were almost opposite. We couldn't help but see a great deal of each other. It wasn't that hard to break down her resistance. My determination eventually paid rewards. Especially when she discovered I was leaving. I'd thought long and hard about moving on. Decided my career was faltering, leaving would be no hardship, my working relationship with Norris ever worsening. I decided my career should continue in ad sales but not with Business Publications.

So I once again became an avid reader of recruitment ads in *Advertising Weekly*. But whatever job I accepted, it would be at a more senior level. Two days later, Pat invited me for an after work drink in the New Victoria pub, alongside the Old Vic Theatre. I accepted. But only if she was paying. "OK. But not if you're wearing that bloody awful black undertaker's overcoat," was her reply.

FOUR

Once again *Advertisers Weekly* came to my rescue. The advertisement for a new publication launch appealed to the requirement I nursed. If successful, I would be the advertising manager of a new monthly, akin to the product areas I had been servicing whilst with Business Publications. Creative Journals were the publishers, domiciled in Grosvenor Street. The chief executive officer was John Ryan. Many moons ago, he had launched Scope, an upmarket business magazine onto an unsuspecting business world. He entered into a business and social partnership with Olive Moore who swiftly adopted the mantle of editor. She was a phenomenally brilliant, hard-hitting journalist, one who pulled no punches. Told it as it was. Spent as much time fighting legal battles as she did putting pen to paper. A truly tough cookie who kept John Ryan on his toes. The next level of employed seniority were yet again a male/female partnership; Charles and Yvonne Fowler. Married. Both actively engaged in advertising sales, both team members – long term.

As advertising manager – I think it was time spent actively selling on *Office Equipment News* that edged a hard-fought battle my way – I reported directly to Charles. We worked well together selling advertisements on the dummy issue. My first order was for six half pages, commencing with the first issue of *Scope Factory and Office Service*. John Ryan personally called me to his office and poured me a large congratulatory whisky.

Both my working and social life were progressing satisfactorily. Patricia and I were two years wed. Being nine months pregnant with Ashley, my first born, she had long since ceased working. We were living in Kent, having purchased a newly built two-bedroom bungalow in Longfield, close to where trainer Fred Winter Snr had his horses stabled. If you arose early enough you could watch his horses training on the gallops. It was our wish once married, no interference from either set of parents. Living where we did, it worked a treat. That is until the night Ashley, who had been particularly restless all week, decided to change his current, comfortable nine-month human abode. But being Ashley, he forgot to inform Pat he was ready to vacate her premises.

When the London Blitz began, I swore I would kill Adolph Hitler plus all his commanders and everything Third Reich. Each member of my boy gang was handpicked by me. Derek Taylor; better known by the nickname of Winkle, given by me for being a wimpy, gutless, tearful, small 'snitch'. He was disliked by each and every one of them. Outlawed. He was only allowed to join my gang in 1947. When Charlton Athletic, the football team we all supported was playing in the 1947 FA Cup, having lost 4–1 to Derby County in extra time the previous year, this time their opponents were Burnley. Three years previous, Winkle's dad had rescued a South African restaurateur from angry dockers unwilling to pay for their meal. He pulled union rank; they paid up and left. Gratitude grew into a strong friendship. One year later, the owner returned to South Africa. Before he went, he actually gave his greasy spoon dockside cafe to Derek's dad. Gobsmacked, he immediately left both the union and his stevedore dock job. He and his wife took over the running of the cafe. It blossomed, as did the Taylors' good fortune. They sold the cafe and bought a local smallholding. In 1947, television was in its infancy. I was desperately trying to discover anybody, a known or unknown acquaintance so wealthily endowed as to own one. You may well ask why.

Since filling my first nappy I had supported Charlton Athletic Football Club. Walking to every home game at the Valley, Charlton's home ground. Clutching the three pence (old money) entrance fee I'd been willingly given by my mum! She loved me to have an interest and football was it. Reaching the 1946 Cup Final was phenomenal for Charlton. I could only listen on the radio. Weep when they were beaten 4–1 in extra time by Derby County. But in answer to my prayers, they were a team possessed the following year. Playing out of their skins. They stunned all of the pundits to appear at Wembley once more. The only way I was going to see this game was on TV. The only TV I was going to watch was – guess whose? You're right first time. The Taylors'. I commenced my overtures to Winkle when Charlton reached the semi-final. Rang him, instead of him ringing me. The Taylors' smallholding was just a few miles from where we lived. My strategy worked. On the Taylors' TV I watched Charlton beat Burnley one nil in the 1947 Cup Final, winger Chris Duffy scoring the winning goal.

Once married and having moved to Longfield, Winkle became an infrequent visitor. I was never able to change my opinion of him. He nearly always arrived unannounced and rarely departed the right side of midnight. Evenings and weekends. Usually alone. But not this evening. Pat was heavily pregnant, told by the midwife to expect Ashley, our first-born, within the week. She had been 'edgy' for the past forty-eight hours. Would you believe that evening at nine o'clock, Winkle Taylor appeared, accompanied by a girl we had never seen before. Both were well oiled. And randy. They practically fell into the hall as I opened the front door. Once in the lounge, they sprawled onto the sofa. Then the snogging commenced in earnest. Pat was absolutely livid. She wanted them gone. So did I. Winkle was having none of it. Requesting glasses, he produced a bottle of wine from his girlfriend's large handbag. By this time, Winkle's hand had long since disappeared under Vera's top. Disgusted, Pat had disappeared into the bedroom. I just sat there in silence, fascinated, wondering just how far this live show would progress before I had to throw them out. That's when nature intervened. Pat called me from the bedroom. Loud enough for Vera's left boob to quickly disappear back into her bra, stopping Winkle in an instant. There was fear and panic in Pat's voice.

"Frank. The baby's coming." I rushed into the bedroom. Already the bed was wet. "I think my waters have broken. Call an ambulance." It was September. My first son was on his way. But the drama was not yet over. There were as yet no communication lines to the new bungalow development on which we were currently living. The only phone was in a phone box a good half-mile away. Portable phones were unheard of. Winkle and Vera, now free of all sexual stimulation, agreed to sit with Pat as I set off for the public phone. It was now one o'clock in the morning. I was seriously out of breath when I delivered my call for an ambulance. I set off back home. Not only had we no telephone, we had no car either. They were helping Pat into the ambulance as I arrived. Pat implored me to go to Dartford Hospital with her. It was eight miles away. I had to walk home. I was halfway there when a very large cow stuck its head through the hedge, at the same time emitting the loudest 'moo' you ever did hear. It might well have been the only way it could offer congratulations. It frightened the crap out of me, literally, making the rest of the journey home decidedly uncomfortable.

FIVE

Whilst it was most gratifying to be a dad and to have a son, Ashley (the name we finally agreed upon following days of in-fighting), he changed the way we had been living. Enormously. My now employment with Creative Journals meant I was out of the office as much as I was in. From the moment Pat returned home, complete with a so-called bundle of joy, I was able to arrange my working days so that I was rarely late home. Much appreciated by my wife. Not so by Lee (as we were now calling him). He did everything expected of a young baby. Beautifully. But every time he opened his eyes, the little bugger's mouth automatically accompanied them. Completely indifferent to the time of day. Or night. It was running Pat ragged. So much so, the moment I walked through the front door a squalling, shawl-wrapped noise machine became my sole possession until neighbours Dorothy and Bob delivered me to the train station next morning. In a matter of weeks I'd aged years. On the night it ended I'd fed him, burped him, bathed him, changed him (twice), laid him in his bed (twice). I whispered whenever conversation was necessary. When it wasn't I sat with my ear glued to the TV screen, the volume was turned so low. Finally I went to bed at 1.25am, exhausted.

As soon as my head hit the pillow, I turned on my right side. Welcomed the land of nod in record time. Then I heard it. That all too familiar sound. I was awake in seconds. Pat wasn't. So I woke her. She argued, so did I. Violently. And won. Lifted Lee from his bed. Laid him at the foot of ours. Crawled back into ours. Turned on my side and it happened. As Pat removed his nappy, his tiny todger stood to attention and he piddled straight over his head, directly into my left ear. I screamed. I could not believe what was happening. Where was the water coming from? I leapt out of bed. Pat was laughing. Uncontrollably. I stormed from the bedroom. Collapsed on the sofa where I slept badly for the rest of the week. How she engineered such a feat of incredible accuracy I'll never know. Sixty-two years on, nor does she.

Apart from such rare mishaps, we lived happily in Longfield until the event of a Peeping Tom. His first appearance was the weekend we entertained Pat's best friend from schooldays. She was another Patricia, as were many if not all women at that time. Once back at the bungalow, the main topic of conversation was clothes. Patricia's fiancé was a serving soldier, stationed at Leicester. He was on a weekend leave and joining Patricia at our bungalow. I'd never met him prior to today. The arrangement was to meet at Victoria Station's pub. We did. I liked him from the start. He offered to buy the first round. Like turned to love. Both on time, we had the first pint at six. The last at seven. We caught the train and then took a taxi to Hart Shaw. Mon repose. On arrival it was dark. So was the bungalow. Apart from the kitchen. The door was locked. Front door too, lights blazing, curtains drawn tight. When I finally persuaded Pat and Patricia that John and I were friends, not foe, the front door was unbolted. We entered to find two frightened young ladies.

Pat was the first to speak. "I thought you were coming straight home. You could have caught the bloke." She went on to explain she was showing Patricia her recently purchased wardrobe. She had only part-pulled the bedroom curtains, to which her back was turned. She asked Patricia's opinion of her latest acquisition. "I think it's lovely," said Patricia. "I bet he does too." Pat spun round and screamed; she was practically face to face with a man whose face was pressed hard against the window. Now Patricia joined in the screaming as the intruder turned tail and fled. Both girls ran into the kitchen, eventually plucking up courage to lock every door and turn off every light.

Once I knew exactly what had taken place, I needed to inform the police. The problem was we were still waiting for our telephone to be connected. So yet again I set off for the red telephone box. Half a mile away. The operator connected me to the local bobby. Or would have done so if he had been home. I almost hung up before a very young voice came on the line. It was his eleven-year-old son. His dad was out with his mum. It was late and he had been in bed. I told him about the intruder, asking him to tell his dad about the Peeping Tom. His reply; "Peeping Tom. Can you spell it please?" Apparently, our PT had become a growing aggravation to the good folk of Longfield. He certainly had to us.

I was on a business trip to Bristol. How he knew, I know not. Perhaps he just got lucky on this occasion. His voyeurism evenings had bypassed us for weeks but on this warm summer's evening, Pat decided upon a relaxing languish in the bath. She left the bathroom window ever-so-slightly on the latch. PT could not believe his luck. Reached in for a full-on view of my naked wife. In return, she had a full-on view of our PT. Consequently, whenever I travelled on business, she went home to Mum who lived in Seven Kings, Essex. A long and difficult journey, especially for a seven months pregnant woman with a young baby. As it looked like our local bobby was destined never to catch the bugger, as much as we loved living there, we moved. I never liked living with Mother-in-Law, Father-in-Law either, but until our Longfield bungalow sold it was our only option.

Once domiciled with Pat's mum and dad, our search for a house began in earnest. We'd enjoyed living at one level in Longfield. Therefore, the management – my pet name for Pat – said any suitable accommodation would suffice provided it was a three- or four-bedroom bungalow. Just when the atmosphere began to react to the overcrowding, Eureka! We came face to face with the answer. A bungalow that ticked all the management's boxes? Older than I would have liked. But well looked after. We had purchased the newly built Longfield bungalow for £2,000. Sold it eighteen months later for £2,200. Then purchased the Upminster bungalow for £2,800. Perhaps I would not have been so keen to buy had I looked before leaping. Believe it or not, living next door were seventeen Pekinese dogs and one Boxer. Pat and I love dogs, as you'll discover later.

You can imagine. Seventeen. Surely, they were housed in garden kennels? Wrong! They lived in the house. Any noise and they were off. A sparrow's fart had them all barking in Pekinese. A cacophony of high-pitched canine excitement. All seventeen. Bursting onto what remained of a lawn. Once green, now a series of patches. Paw deep in dog poo. It made you wonder what might have greeted you indoors. I had no desire to find out. And never did.

Ron, their son, and Carol, his wife, lived on the other side of us. We got on fine. They were very embarrassed about the dogs. And the noise they made, knowing we had young children. Also the ever present smell. Ron tried so very hard to keep his parents back garden poo-free. It was a thankless task. He tried even harder once our second son was born. As it happened, he needn't have worried. Within a week of moving in, I knew it was a mistake. There and then I began the task of finding the means of moving out. It took some considerable time finding a suitable property in the same area. I'm not a person that gives in easily, but fifteen months later I was becoming despondent.

Then it happened. One of the three estate agents I had briefed concerning my living requirements rang. His son came home from school upset. His best friend said they were moving to the seaside, soon. They currently lived in Hornminster Glen, a cul-de-sac just behind where we were living in Minster Way. He would be calling upon them the next day. If their impending move were true, would it be of interest? Would it? I told him if it were true he could double his fee. Within the week it was ours. For £3,600. A delightful three-bedroom end-of-row house. The daughter we both wanted was born there. I came close to being 'nicked' there. But then again that's another story. It was our home for the next fifteen years. We sold it for £65,000.

It was one of a recent development of modern three/four-bedroom semi-detached spacious bungalows. Ashley reached his first birthday there. Two joint decisions were made. His first birthday present from his mum and dad would be a dog. A loveable Golden Retriever we named Amber, loved by everyone who crossed her path. The only one of fifteen dogs we actually paid for. All of the other fourteen we rescued. Including

Bonnie, the only dog we have now. An eighteen-month-old brutalised Romanian street dog. The charity who rescued her said she had just two more days to live before being put down. By humane injection? Nothing so humane. She was likely to be clubbed to death, so the charity said. So please, if any reader is thinking of dog rescue, before doing so contact Saving Romanian Strays. Have a look online?

Bonnie brought the total number of dogs we have rescued to date to fifteen. The most we have ever had at one time was five. They included a Parsons Jack Russell and an Irish Wolfhound.

The Wolfhound had been taken to Brentwood Police Station. Found in a man's front garden, she weighed just four stone; had no coat and a body smothered in abscesses; had only one eye and was terrified of human beings. The police rushed her to the Blackmore Vet where my daughter worked. They said she would have to be put down. Nic, my daughter, pleaded for her life. Night and day, she became her private nurse. She had a good RSPCA friend and discussed what had happened with him. She did not believe the story. Nor did he. Together they decided to visit the neighbours of the man, he who said he had found her in his front garden. The neighbours said that was a pack of lies from start to finish. It was his dog and he treated her abominably. He had another dog, a GSD; it was allowed to live in the house. The Irish Wolfhound was kept in the garden. She had no kennel and was rarely fed. Forced to steal bread and other foods from nearby shops. The neighbours met us in a local pub. Why? Because he was bad tempered, violent and had not spoken to any of his neighbours for years. Once they had given statements confirming the above, the RSPCA issued a court order against him. He failed to appear. A summons was then issued and this frightened him into appearing in court. He was found guilty of cruelty, neglect and ill-treatment of Kylie, the name we had given the Wolfhound, fined £80.00 and banned from keeping any animals for ten years.

A disappointing result. Especially as he already had another dog. One of the neighbours had confessed he treated her very well. The RSPCA said they would ensure he did. My daughter would make certain the promises made, were kept. With Nic nursing Kylie back to health, so began a search for a suitable new home and owner. In the time that had elapsed Kylie made a remarkable recovery. She now weighed eight-and-a-half stone, her true weight. Every one of her body abscesses had disappeared. Her coat had fully re-grown. Sadly, we could do nothing about her missing eye. I suggested we re-named her Nelson. Nic was not amused. Because the country was suffering the worst recession ever (1989/92), finding a suitable new owner was proving impossible. It seems nobody wanted the financial burden of a dog now weighing eight-and-a-half stone.

Then it began. Non-stop pleading from all of my family to let Kylie come and live with us. Having been given a clean bill of health, the vets wanted her gone. They needed the space. Why couldn't she come and live with us until her new home was found? The answer was simple. We already had four dogs, all rescued, living with us. Surely that's enough. It seems not. She arrived forty-eight hours later. Very soon, she and I were inseparable. We did everything together. Including watching TV. Me in my chair, her with her bum in my lap, her long front legs on the floor. She ran like a rocking horse, playing all sorts of doggy games both indoors and out with all of her four canine companions. Never an angry bark. Ever. I was hopelessly in love with her. She was about six when she moved in. We had three incredible years together. Then came the cancer. Terminal. I had to call the vet. Her head cradled in my arms. Her single eye never left my face. She gently licked my hand. This was goodbye. She died. People say big boys don't cry. Don't believe it. They do. I did. This was her epitaph. Her memory lives on.

*

I stood beside your bed last night, you found it hard to sleep.
I wiped away a silent tear and begged you not to weep
I whispered to you softly, I'm with you have no fear
I haven't really left you. I'm well, I'm fine, I'm here
I was close to you at breakfast, but that you could not see.
Thinking of the many times your hand reached down to me.
I was with you at my grave today, you tend it with such care

How can I reassure you; I'm not really lying there?
It's possible for me to be so close to you each day
If only I could let you know I never went away
You sat there very quietly, you smiled as if you knew
In the stillness of each evening, I'm so very close to you
And when the time is right for you, to cross the brief divide
I'll be waiting there to greet you, never more to leave your side.

(Anon)

*

During the fifteen years we lived in Hornminster Glen, my business life progressed as planned. Whilst with Creative Journals, John Ryan, no longer a young man, sold the company. Lock, stock and barrel. The buyers were a very progressive Canadian company called McLean Hunter, headquartered in Toronto, keen to develop a publishing foothold in the UK. We were it. As you would expect, I was anxious about my future with a company I, and my colleagues, knew virtually nothing about except that they were a major Canadian publishing force. They had already appointed an English chief executive officer. Ron Barnes. From whence he came I know not. He was to introduce us to Canadian working practices wherein each existing publication would have its own publisher totally responsible for the success – or failure – of his or her publication. In the time I spent with them, the first female publisher had yet to be appointed.

I loved the name the moment I heard it. Theodore van Beek. He was the managing director. The only man to have fired me. Ever. I was the advertising manager of *Business Systems & Equipment*. My publisher was Jimmy James. He was truly a gentleman. A lovely, lovely man and a delight to report to. Taking everything into account, all in all, it was a happy ship. Any existing problems were quickly removed. New publishing practices introduced, one of which was to set up a Salesman of the Year award. In my sales career to date, I never did other than work bloody hard. Consequently, my salary was adequate to the demands of a wife, three children, nice house, mortgage, comfortable lifestyle. So once told the rules pertaining to the Salesman of the Year award, I decided to give it a crack. Publishers could not enter. Jimmy made certain, where possible, potential new advertisers were allocated to me. In the final furlong it was neck and neck between *Modern Purchasing, British Printer* and me.

I had two new advertisers. Both told me *BS&E* would be included on this year's schedules. It was touch and go. God bless them. Both reacted to my last-minute telephone call explaining the situation. Both came good. Their orders for full and half pages arrived. There were just three days left. When all total individual advertising revenues were totalled, I was the winner. By a whisker. Soon after, I thanked Jimmy over lunch at the Vecchia Riccone, my very favourite London Italian restaurant. I loved working for McLean Hunter. They were full of surprises. If Jimmy James had been allowed to enter the Salesman of the Year competition, then he would have won. Comfortably. Having him as my publisher was an education, but the CEO had other ideas. He saw Jimmy as a trouble shooter. A fire fighter. With little warning he was removed from *Business Systems & Equipment* and given sole charge of a magazine that had been losing revenue for the best part of a year. He was given a year to break even. Did it in eight months and it was profitable by Christmas.

I understand on Jimmy's say-so I was strongly recommended as his successor, thanks to working alongside him since day one. He convinced Ron Barnes I was good and ready. I must was have done the same during my interview with him. I was now the youngest ever McLean Hunter publisher, either side of the Atlantic. My publication was solidly established. Each issue producing expanding profit. I had a senior salesman. I was certain we would reach my targeted monthly advertising revenue quicker if I could appoint a second salesman. I was told I could do so by Theo van Beek but I had to reach a 65 per cent annual advertising revenue first.

Jimmy was now out of the equation. I'd arranged the lunch to thank him for everything; I owed him a king's ransom. The lunch was accompanied by pints. Pints of pints. Followed by brandies. Time had no relevance. I was repaying a debt of honour. Jimmy looked at his watch. Stood up. Announced he was going to the loo.

Carried on home. His was a long journey. He lived in Brighton. Mine was short. It was five o'clock. Foolishly I headed back to Savile Row, my office. Once inside. I virtually collapsed in my chair. Only to be awoken by an apoplectic Van Beek screaming my name. Slowly I realised I was under my desk. In my drunken stupor I must have thought it the best place to recover without being seen.

Earlier I told you Van Beek was the only person to have fired me. It happened there and then. Me flat on my back. Theo on his knees. I was an idiot. Like Jimmy, I should have gone straight home. Even Theo said so when he was reinstating me in his office next morning. I still cringe mentally whenever I recall that day. Having been given the CEO's approval to advertise for a second salesman needed to assist in reaching my revised advertising revenue – you've guessed it – the first applicant had been sitting in my office since three-thirty. The poor sod was then transferred to Theo's office. He did the interview. Then left a message with my secretary that I was to report to him the moment I appeared. Instead, anger mounting, he came looking for me. At six-fifteen I was jobless. Fired by the managing director.

I phoned Jimmy later at home. By the time I reached the office next morning, Ron Barnes and Theo had both been seen by Jim. He told each in turn it was his fault. Not mine. It was to thank me for the lions' share of Business Systems successful first year. I sent a personal memo of apology to both. In return, Theo told me the applicant he saw wasn't suitable. As well as working hard for long periods, with rewards equal to efforts made, I also took calculated risks. But the overpowering desire to be my own boss grew ever stronger as I grew older. So, I took chances with smaller independent publishers as well as house magazines published by associations, one of which was the *Chartered Mechanical Engineer*. I worked alongside the editor, Eric Semler. Then, when I felt I knew just about everything CMEs were and did, their role in industry, the companies that belonged, the achievements, history, I said my farewell. Thanked them all for three happy years. Then I was gone. Leaving the publication with constantly improving advertising revenues.

SIX

At this stage in my life I started playing golf. Badly. Then I spotted it. A magazine called *Golfing*, in urgent need of an advertising manager. I did as the advertisement suggested, rang the number given. It was a Caterham number; I lived in Upminster, a long way from Caterham. The lady I was talking to suggested I made an appointment with Gordon Binns. He owned *Golfing*. The following Tuesday I was sitting opposite this man. He seemed nervous. He gave me a copy of *Golfing*. It was pitifully short of paid advertising. From there on it seemed I was running the interview. I gave him a potted history of my career to date, told him the salary I wanted, the car I wanted. A London office (I had already agreed with a friend to rent space in his Soho Square premises). Expenses. Three weeks' paid holiday. He agreed to all of my terms. In return, I told him I would probably be able to quadruple *Golfing*'s current advertising revenue within the first year. We shook hands. I left feeling this was going to be the best job ever.

Ouch! I was a big boy. Got rather carried away. I really should have known better. Before I joined *Golfing* as advertising manager there were things I needed to know. I bought every golfing magazine published in the UK and studied each respectively. It seemed each one had the advertising volume its editorial and layout deserved. I was also able to make comparisons with randomly selected copies of *Golfing*. Sadly there were few comparisons to be made. It was obvious advertisers in *Golfing* were offered ridiculous discounts for series bookings. This Gordon denied. I knew differently. The road ahead was going to be next to impossible. It was. I commenced my employment the month the Open was to be played in Turnberry, Scotland. Gordon flew to the course hotel. I was to join him there.

It so happened that night Brian Curvis of Wales was challenging Emil Griffiths, USA for his world boxing crown. I was going to the fight with a bunch of Croydon publicans, staying overnight in London and flying to Scotland early next morning, being picked up at the airport by Gordon, then back to the course hotel. To a shared room. This, I thought, was not a good idea. It was a bad night. It showed the vast difference in class between British and American champions. Curvis, who up to then was unbeaten, was game but outclassed.

With little else to offer, he was stopped in round four. Feeling badly let down by the British Champion, it was all back to Norman's pub in Croydon. I only bought one round, intending not to stay but foolishly downed the contents of at least eight more. I needed cheering up. I should have woken in my London hotel. Instead, I opened my eyes as I rolled off the settee in a four-ale pub in downtown Croydon. Still as drunk as a skunk with precious little time to leg it to the airport, feeling like death, wishing it would come for me. Now!

I made it by the skin of my hangover. Feeling I would throw up with every running step, I just made the rear aircraft boarding ramp. I spied an empty seat at the rear of the aircraft, next to an elderly bloke nodding off and wakened him as I fell into the empty seat. He was none too pleased. I turned to apologise. Shock. Horror. It was the 'Wakey, Wakey' man himself. None other than Billy Cotton Snr, radio's unbelievably popular band leader. I felt embarrassingly stupid and apologised profusely. By now, the cabin staff had arrived in numbers and said they would remove me. He was having none of it. Sent them packing. Said as I smelt like a brewery he wanted to know why. I explained I was at the Curvis fight with a bunch of publicans. He stopped me there and wanted my opinion of the fisticuffs. Like me, he thought Curvis unbeatable, which he was until this fight. All the time we were talking, he was popping pills. Suddenly he smiled. When I asked why, he said one word; "Brooklands."

The plane was flying over the once globally famous motor racing track. He'd raced there as a young man, the happiest time in his wonderful life. Whilst recounting his motor racing experiences, the smile never once left his face. He was Scotland-bound at the invitation of Harry Lauders' widow. Harry, now dead, 'Keep Right On To The End Of The Road' his signature tune. A world-renowned Scottish comedian. They regularly shared the same stage, the same bill, and became firm friends. Now retired, when the going got tough now and again Bill found the time to visit Harry's wife and loved it. His last words as we touched down were, "I hope the bloody press vultures don't spoil it." They already had. Five of them waiting on the tarmac, two with cameras, waiting for Bill to disembark. Bill, still sitting in his seat, a sick, elderly and much-loved popular band leader, seeking just a few days' solitude shared with the widow of an equally much-loved Scottish show-biz friend, hoping the press would go away. But knowing the buggers wouldn't. They never did.

The two days spent by Gordon's side emphasised *Golfing* was a no-no. A greater mistake than choosing to live next door to seventeen yappy, crappy Pekinese dogs. The only relief I had was when he arranged interviews with players. Mainly American. Or when he wanted to report on needle matches, giving me the chance to gauge the opinion of *Golfing*. It was not good, I soon realised. Telling Gordon I would quadruple advertising revenue in twelve months – that was a mistake. However hard I tried the problem was readily recognisable. Its owner. And having given up on miracles a long time since, by asking questions, Gordon's history before and after he purchased the magazine was revealed. His family wealth was built on the woollen industry. Gordon was its main beneficiary, enabling him to purchase *Golfing*. Outright. In less than a year it was struggling. Mentally, he was far from a well man as I was soon to discover. As my salary was good, I could afford to stay with *Golfing* for six months. That was my vanity. Speaking out of turn.

SEVEN

On my return from Scotland there was a telephone message from Grace Tony AP's PA. He would like to see me. Preferably over lunch. I knew little of him, only that he was the young managing director of Beacon Advertising and associates, an agency started by his father, in Manchester. Eventually moving south via Twickenham, settling in Bromley, Kent. From day one they had concentrated on technical accounts. Those, mostly other northern-based agencies, purposely gave the cold shoulder. Giving AP's dad his due, he had fire in his belly. Saw the opportunity. Put his creative talents to growing technical demands. Opened his own Manchester-based advertising agency. Offering a range of much-needed technical advertising services under one roof. A shrewd move. Like little Topsy, it grew and grew. Why AP, his son, was appointed managing director, I could never understand, whilst I believed moving south enabled them to pitch for more than technical accounts. Some of the agency personnel came south too. I called on the agency fairly often. They had accounts advertising in the *Mechanical Engineer*. After I lunched with AP I could see his problem. His brother-in-law, the only company employee of AP's age, had handed in his notice. The other account-handling executives were much older. So were the creative and copywriting staff.

But the biggest problem was the father, as I discovered all too soon. He was now in Malta, looking after and living on board a yacht. Not just any old yacht, but the one belonging to the advertising director of The Sunday Times Newspaper Group. He was skippering the yacht as and when wealthy clients hired it. Nothing wrong with that, I agree! But having said yes to running the Maltese yacht hire business, promising AP not to interfere with his running of Peers Advertising, then doing nothing else but. I knew nothing of this.

Sitting opposite AP and his PA Grace, in my favourite London Italian restaurant, I was being propositioned. New business director. Excellent salary. Choice of company car. Commission on new business written. Three weeks' annual holiday. It was both flattering and timely. The six months' trial I was prepared to give *Golfing* was nearing its end. The golfing fraternity I met in Scotland thought I was mad, or stupid, firmly believing *Golfing* would not be around in six months.

Whenever Gordon and golfing's heavyweights were in close proximity, hostility was never far away. I returned home alone. Gordon then disappeared. There was still no London office. No company car. I was expected to travel to the office three days a week. I told him OK, once I had a car. Without one I needed two trains and the London Underground. Time taken; two-and-a-half-hours, Galleywood to Caterham.

His mental situation was in free fall. It was seven o'clock Friday morning. Gordon was on the phone. He urgently needed to see me. I decided I would go and tell him what needed to happen. If then he didn't agree, I was leaving. I drove Pat's car. Thank God I did. There in an untidy pile were all my personal belongings, piled high in the street. I was livid. He wasn't there. I drove home profanely cursing Gordon Binns. I never spoke to him again. It wasn't long after I discovered he had died in hospital.

EIGHT

The first thing I did when I arrived home was to call Grace. "When do I start?" was all I said. I'd been given a month to consider joining Beacon Advertising. A month of broken *Golfing* promises. A month when a little voice from my inner self kept repeating *You shouldn't have joined, you silly bugger. You shouldn't have joined.* I had. And regretted it almost immediately. Beacon advertising was a totally different ball game. Selling advertising space since leaving the Royal Air Force had connected me with a great number of advertising agencies, large and small, also those in other major cities. Whilst I preferred selling direct to the advertiser, I also made certain I had built strong, friendly business contacts with agency personnel handling these accounts. How strong and friendly was about to be put to the test.

Through Grace I was able to persuade AP to throw a 'meet the new boy' party for selective agencies. Those whose accounts we already managed. Or wished to. He was under orders to ring his father each week with a 'to date' what's happening report. Without telling Grace or me, he told his dad about the party. Without telling AP, Dad turned up. Well and truly oiled. I focused on AP's face as his father walked – nay, practically fell – through the door. Shock. Horror. Despair. The party was planned to run from six to eight. We had just entered the final furlong. As the evening had progressed, Grace and I agreed it had visibly achieved what it set out to achieve. She was magnificent, AP disappointing. Having introduced me as the new kid on the block, he spent the rest of the evening in the company of the agency's three largest clients. She warned me this would happen. It did. The agency's MD/PA's roles reversed. She introduced me to those she knew (practically all the guests). I reversed the situation with those I knew. In the few short weeks I had been Beacon Advertising new business director, it was obvious to me Grace was running the show. She told me later she'd had a recurring premonition that dad would gatecrash the party, even though he had told AP he wouldn't.

Fortunately, the party was nearing its end. We both agreed it had the desired result. Those left were, in the, main, our people or clients of long standing, well used to dad's behaviour when drunk. Which he was. Whatever he had planned on doing, now, escorted by Grace, remained undone. The Bloomsbury apartment we were in was owned by the company. It's where he stayed when in London as Beacon Advertising was based in Bromley, Kent. It was further utilised for meetings with London-based clients, also potential and existing client marketing and PR campaigns. In the few years I stayed with the agency, Bloomsbury served me well. Clients too were duly impressed. There were times I believed they were the most helpful, adding important new business to the agency's client list. Grace was the only one I told of impending potential new business/existing client meetings. I knew then AP and AP's dad would never gatecrash any of my meetings. Unless invited. Incidentally, AP's greeting when we were introduced was "So you're the whizz-kid come to fill his boots with my money. Just help yourself like the rest of this lot." My reply; "Thanks. But I warn you, I've got bloody big feet." Grace surprised me as I drove back to Essex. "Do you know Frank, that man can empty a room faster than a fart in a phone box."

Whilst working with Beacon, we found and moved to a new four-bedroom property in Galleywood, Essex. It was owned by Mr Teahon who ran a general hardware shop in Ilford. By this time, Nic was keen to add a 14.2 hand horse to Fonz, the small 11.2 hand gymkhana pony she had long-since outgrown. Apart from four bedrooms, two bathrooms and large garden, attached were two wildly overgrown acres included in the asking price of £84,000. I paid £78,000. Contracts were exchanged. Moving-in dates agreed. Everything was set fair. Or so we thought. It was then Teahon proved just how crooked he was. A week before we were due to move, Barry who owned Silver Carpets gave me an excellent price to carpet two of the bedrooms. I rang the estate agent for the keys, only to be told they did not have them. Nor did I have Teahon's telephone number. Or the name or address of his general store. Moving day arrived. So did the removal van.

Years previously, we agreed if Pat's parents decided to sell their Seven Kings Essex house then the money raised would be used to build a one-bedroom extension to the side of our Galleywood house. Any shortfall in the money needed I would supply. Planning permission was readily granted. True to their word, the builders kept to their building schedule. Pat's mum and dad were now living alongside. Any money shortfall I made good, considering it acceptable. Especially in relation to the value it added to the house. The disadvantage; Sylvia. Mother-in-law. An embittered, spiteful old lady. She was the youngest in her family. She met Jack, Pat's father when he was still married. You've guessed it. She fell pregnant! The year; 1937. She gave birth to a daughter. The only one pleased was me – I married her. The rest of her family never forgave her. Hence the bitterness until the day she died. So, can you really blame her?

The Galleywood house had comfortably accommodated Sylvia, along with Pat and me and three children. This meant there were excessive goods and chattels to move. In fact, by 9.30am, the contents of two houses were loaded and ready to travel the short journey to our new home. But there were still no bloody keys. I can no longer remember who gave us the address in Southend where the keys were located. Cursing Teahon, I instructed the estate agent where they were. At last I would be able to unlock the door and enter our new home. The first thing that shocked me as I entered the hall was the large number of gin bottles. Empty gin bottles. Thirty-eight of them. Considering he told me he only spent one night a week at the house, he must have had one hell of a prodigious thirst. Once inside I climbed the stairs. The mirror fitting the whole of one en-suite tiled bathroom wall. Gone. Ripped from the wall. The tiles badly damaged. The deep-pile master bedroom and landing carpet. Stolen. Now I knew why Teahon refused to give me the keys when first I asked. Neither did it end there. Having checked every room thoroughly, I decided to open the locked garage doors. That is if the keys could be found. I should have known. They were nowhere to be found. Not wanting to damage the locking mechanism of double garage doors, a locksmith had to be called. I have never seen a double garage so crammed to the ceiling with rubbish. It took me and the whole of my family twelve trips to the tip before it was emptied. I was furious. Even more so when I came across return flight ticket stubs in the piles of discarded paperwork. To and from Barbados. As I stared at them there was murder in my heart. I vowed to get the bastard into court. It took a little time but the papers were eventually served. Would you believe whilst sitting and awaiting the Payne v. Teahon case to be called, my gaze never left his face. He had a lady lawyer defending him. She, he and I all knew he was guilty. Suddenly she was bearing down on Pat and I. Teahon knew he was on a hiding to nothing. Told his brief to offer £1,500 in full and final out of court settlement. Not wishing to appear rude, I asked her to tell him "to stick his offer up his arse". I left court smiling broadly, £4,600 better off, having listened to the Judge's opinion of Teahon. I hung on to every scathing word. It felt good. Justice had been done.

NINE

Grace Davis was a diamond. Why she joined Beacon I will never know. After only a short while, I was of the opinion she, and AP, should have exchanged roles in the agency's hierarchy. In the first eighteen months I had won five new accounts. I was asked if I wanted my own secretary. I did not. And said so. My working arrangement with Grace suited me admirably. I trusted her implicitly, as did each of my new client contacts. She sat in meetings between AP and me. Also, the infrequent board meetings AP called. But for me her handling of AP was priceless. I'm sure she should have entered politics, not advertising.

I'm convinced AP was in awe of his father. I therefore presume his dad's new lifestyle was being financed by the agency. Why not? After all, he would tell anybody who cared to listen, it was his blood, sweat and tears that set the wheels in motion. He and he alone made Beacon the success of yesteryear. The longer I worked for them, the more I relied on Grace. Two years on, she had become as close to my accounts as me. In fact, I honestly think they loved and preferred it. AP didn't. I could foresee he worried increasingly that I would leave, taking my accounts and Grace with me. It was something that crossed my mind, infrequently, as the increasing traffic between Galleywood and Bromley became heavier and more and more tiresome.

Being a gentleman, I never once asked Grace her age. But I guessed she was in her early to mid-forties. She dressed immaculately, seemed to have boundless energy and nothing ever fazed her. I regularly referred to her as my 'smiling saviour'. In the years we worked together, she never once let me down. She always looked a picture of health. Never once had a day off sick. Yet she had terminal cancer. I never knew. Her husband, rang in saying she was taking a few days' leave. Feeling a little off colour. She died that weekend. It was the news that greeted me when I arrived at the office on Monday. I could hardly hold back the tears. I went back to my car. The fond memories came flooding in. Without exception, male or female, Grace was the loveliest person I'd ever had the good fortune to work with. It was a day I spent ringing all of my clients. They found the news hard to accept. How would I replace her? I used one word to each. Irreplaceable. Both in the office and in my heart. Without exception, every client sent flowers to the funeral. It took me a long time to come to terms with the tragedy. If the truth were known, I never did.

The other bad news I received that Monday was that AP's dad was returning from Malta. For good. Taking up residence in the Bloomsbury flat. The alarm bells were ringing from that moment on. Subconsciously, when Grace died, the thought of leaving Beacon changed. From being perhaps, when the time is right, to thinking would it be prudent to go it alone. Which of my accounts would go with me? I decided to drop gentle hints now that Grace was gone. Gauge the reaction to my suggestions. My fears that things would change with the return of AP's dad, he would not stand up to him, nor support me if and when I did. Neither would any of the old timers.

I had no intention of watching him ruining what I had built over three years. I had hoped that with my backing, AP's would not be bullied. But then again, leopards and spots. Sadly, he made no effort at all to prevent my worst fears coming true. My notice was handed in six months later. Within the first year with Beacon. I was disenchanted overall with much of the creative work produced. Or rather, the lack of it. Particularly where the new accounts were concerned. It was, in my opinion, 'ordinary', and the cause of continual disagreements between AP and myself. Latterly I had to argue to use freelance artists from a young up-and-coming graphics studio I was introduced to by John. His brother was one of the six artists operating as a limited company. I used them when I was the publisher (the youngest ever) of *Business Systems & Equipment*.

Eventually, and with Grace in my corner, we persuaded AP to bring them into my new business presentations. With them, we won more than we lost. I had agreed a special rate with them. This allowed Beacon to satisfactorily increase their cost to client and me to use them where and when I considered it necessary. They were called Shape. They were to play an ever-increasing role in my future business life.

*

Most people when asked "Have you ever seen a badger?" reply, "Yes. Sadly, dead in the road." When asked that question Pat and I would almost certainly have given that answer too. That is until we moved to our new house in Galleywood. The house was newly built and had hardly been lived in. It occupied one hectare (two acres) of land. Terribly overgrown with seven-foot nettles, brambles and all things wild. Once cleared, I had it fenced. Divided into two one-acre paddocks, divided by a five-bar gate. Then I had a four-stable block built. Our smallholding was surrounded by 176 acres of orchard, the owners of which made us most welcome. We asked, and were given, permission to walk our dogs there. The first time Pat walked them, she said she had seen positive signs of badgers. Later, when she asked

Steven, the owner, his answer to her question was in the affirmative. "I don't know how many but quite a few." Steven, Philip and their father owned this and three other orchards in the immediate proximity. They were quite happy for Pat to badger-watch any evening. Any orchard. But now Pat had seen definite signs of badgers, with only a hedge separating them from us, she was determined to encourage them into our garden. You won't believe how she achieved it. You certainly won't believe the end result.

Once Pat knew there were badgers almost within touching distance, she decided they should be this side of the hedge too. Within cuddling distance. So the planning began. She had me clear three different floor level gaps in the orchard hedge. Then, early every evening, off to the kitchen she trotted, emerging thirty minutes later with a pile of strawberry jam, peanut butter, chocolate spread and Marmite sandwiches. Each sandwich neatly quartered. They were accompanied by a selection of various biscuits. Mainly Rich Tea and Jammy Dodgers. Occasionally, she made them cakes too. Then we sat in the lounge. Waiting for 10.30pm to be signalled by the alarm clock. She had insisted on the alarm in case we nodded off. Then, with an uncanny sense of punctuality, the badger(s) arrived for supper. If there was none, she believed they would run off, never to return. So said the provider of the feast. As she never nodded off – I often did – the theory was never put to the test.

At Pat's instruction, the hedge gaps were positioned at the end of the garden inviting the badger(s) to investigate our quite large garden for other goodies. So we laid three trails of enticing food, starting the orchard side of the hedge. Once inside our garden, the three merged into one. This ran down the garden to the back of the house. That's where the majority of the food was spread giving full view of however many badgers came to supper. We waited, waited, and waited. We watched from ten o'clock through a whole range of different times until late into the early hours. We saw no sign of cunning Mr Brock.

Yet when we awoke and went into the garden, there was a carpet of crumbs. Little holes full of badger poo – the universal way badgers mark their territory. With our garden now claimed as badger country, Pat was sure we were on the verge of a sighting. Glory be! She was right. It was just before midnight. Without any sighting of anything, I decided enough was enough. It was cold. My bed was calling. Pat was standing behind a large apple tree about twenty feet from the piece of lawn known as Badger's Cafe. I was halfway through the French windows, then I heard it. Half-strangled, Pat calling my name. "Frank. Look!" I turned. Slowly. Not wanting to frighten whatever it was Pat had seen. Now I saw it. Keeping the hedge close should danger appear, a bold young badger. Directly in front of Pat, less than fifteen feet from the apple tree, feeding hungrily. Looking directly at Pat's hiding place. He (or she) sensed her presence. Both of us hardly dared to breathe. Being alone, the adventurous young badger took his fill of Pat's table. Then, relaxed and well fed, slowly retraced his footsteps and was gone from whence he or she came. Pat was excited. Thrilled. Elated. As well she should be. Her patience had paid a priceless reward, the one she had worked so tirelessly to achieve.

Then, false alarm. Our solo visitor did not come back. Even though Pat continued with her nightly feeding. Disappointment grew with each of the six nights of badger absence. Then seven proved to be our lucky number. Not one but three badgers, led by our first-night friend. They came stealthily through the hedge, eating their determined way down each of the three footpaths. Only stopping when they arrived at the enticing picnic on the lawn. From that day until we sold up and moved away from Galleywood, we would never again have a badgerless night. The numbers continued to grow to a head count you won't believe from our very first shy visitor. The number finally grew to *eleven*. I swear Pat could have fed them by hand. We were able to stand within feet of them in the garden as they ate. You could watch them arrive and wait for Pat to deliver the food. Bold as brass. They would come onto the patio and peer through the large garden windows, hoping more goodies would arrive. The food was delivered at ten o'clock; if late, they would sit or lie in wait. We were able to change the answer to those who had only ever seen their badgers lying dead on the road. They were invited to 'badger watch' where ours were very much alive and kicking. Magic in the making. Pat looked at me triumphantly. Her only comment; "I told you it would be Well Worth Waiting For."

TEN

The atmosphere between AP and myself worsened with every passing day. So much so I was now virtually working from home. Travelling to Bromley once or twice weekly. The time had come for me to go. The oldest account executive had left to run a bookshop in Cheltenham. He said if it were true AP's dad was returning, it was time for his departure. He was gone within the month. With no Grace there to look after me, the writing was on the wall. The accounts I had brought to the agency, whose every need I had personally serviced, wanted to be kept in touch with the developing situation. I had gauged those I was confident would move their accounts. Those who might. Those who wouldn't. Now all I had to do was to settle on the most convenient date of departure. Whilst doing so, a saying I was familiar with entered my mind. Then refused to depart. It was; 'Ageing is compulsory. Growing up is optional.' AP's dad refuses to admit he's old with nothing more of value to give. AP is infantile and will never grow up.

Before I'd given further serious thought to my farewell, I received a letter. It came from Tony. It was a mistake. In his letter I was accused of irresponsibility. Lack of loyalty, plus other offences I had no recollection of. The phone call came from Shape Studio. Could I attend an Ingatestone evening meeting? Intrigued, I arrived at their offices at six-thirty. There were six artists in attendance, combined skills ranging from graphic design to finished artwork. They had all worked individually as freelance artists for Ford Motor Company. How did I come to know of them? When I was a publisher for McLean Hunter, John Mcgowan was selling advertising space on *Business Systems & Equipment*. His brother Ian was one of the six. For quite some time, he had argued for the protection offered by registering the group as a limited company. This they did soon after John told me of them. From the very beginning, I was delighted with the innovation of original design, together with quality of finished artwork. I used them whenever I could. Now I was on my own, I told them I would pass all my advertisement and brochure design/artwork to them. I would only ask that they be prepared to wait for their money until my clients paid me. It's long been known that small suppliers, of which I was one, were historically always last to be paid.

Therefore, I wondered if this evening's meeting would touch on this. Touch on it! Touch. The offer on the table was a knockout blow. When I picked myself off the deck, I was mightily pleased. After Ian opened the meeting with a business resume of how well Shape had fared, as the year's end drew ever closer, he wished to thank me for the substantial chunk of this new business. The amount surprised me. And in Shape's eyes that made me a hero. My reward? If the terms were right, would I join Shape Advertising & Publicity Limited as managing director? I was mega chuffed. Absolutely over the moon. Now it was dependent on my reaction. Would I accept or decline the offer on the table? Of the six partners, four had voted that I should be approached. I asked for fourteen days to consider my decision. This would be ample time enough to appraise them of the terms I wanted if I was to agree. The two who voted against the offer asked my opinion and said they would remain, but only if Shape stayed an independent unit. If not, they would both leave. They duly resigned and left when I said I favoured Shape's new limited company status. The meeting ended there and then. Would I care to join them in their Ingatestone local? A suggestion I accepted, but only if I could buy the first round. It wasn't the only surprise of the evening. Five pints later I shook the hand of my new directors, then left for home.

It was shortly after the new drink/driving laws had been introduced. I gave scant thought to them during the few miles drive to my Galleywood home.

But knowing I was probably over the limit, I took it easy driving down the hill between Upminster and Hornchurch. It was around ten o'clock. Little traffic to be seen. Thinking only of the Shape offer, which I had silently accepted the moment it had been made, I failed to notice the police car close behind me. It was only when the blue lights flashed, I knew I had a police escort. We were under the railway bridge so I pulled over to let them pass. As they did the driver signalled for me to pull in behind them. I did as I was asked, stopped, turned off the engine, applied the handbrake. Sat and waited. Watched the officer carefully position his hat, open the car door, get out, march purposefully toward my car where I remained seated. His opening words were, "Good evening motorist. Been celebrating?" Now I don't know why but the officer who remained in their car was beginning to look remarkably familiar.

Then recognition struck. It was David Jones' dad. "Yes I have Officer. Ask your colleague. He knows me. His son David's a bloody good footballer. He plays for Langton Royals. I'm their manager."

A long silence ensued. "Have you been drinking, Sir?" asked the first officer. "Of course I have. Your colleague Derek knows I like a drink. Or three. Or four or more. Go and ask him." He took my advice. But only after the driving officer got out of the police car, from the full-on frontal I had, he was nothing like Derek Jones. The officer standing beside me ordered me to get into the passenger seat of my car. He then climbed into the driving seat. When I asked why I could not drive he answered, "You're lucky. We were finished for the night and on our way home. Then we saw you driving erratically. Also, you're pissed. And you know it." We were nigh on opposite Hornminster Glen, where I lived. He turned right as I pointed out my house. As he was about to stop I cheekily asked, "Could you park it in the drive please." He looked at me evenly and said, "You're one cheeky, lucky bastard," climbed into the police car and was gone. I could do nowt but agree. I would have been guilty if I'd blown into the bag. They knew it. I knew it. I also knew it would have considerably delayed their end-of-shift departure. They didn't want that. I most certainly didn't.

ELEVEN

I had left Beacon with few regrets, excited and keen to take up my new position with Shape at the end of the month. They had been operating out of Ingatestone. Small but sufficient offices, suitable for the present. At the same time making a mental note we would be gone to bigger premises in eighteen months. Most people refer to the village as 'Ingatestone'. Most people are wrong. 'Ing' is a parcel of land whose boundaries are measured and marked by four large stones. Three have been found. The fourth is believed buried in the village churchyard. The correct pronunciation therefore is 'Ingatstone'.

There was sufficient room for the artists and also a small office for me. Before I joined Shape, they had a part-time accountant by the name of June. She did a good job, keeping the finances of Shape in order. At the end of the first general meeting, it was agreed she be offered the full-time position of Company Secretary. She was delighted to accept. We were well pleased with her acceptance. Frank W. Payne. Managing Director. Shape Advertising & Publicity Ltd. Turnover £235,000. Taken on board to skipper the ship to a turnover of one million pounds plus within the next eighteen months. My target figure. Not theirs. All but one of my accounts followed me to Shape, the one which had recently appointed a new Head of Publicity. We met soon after he joined the company. I left the meeting knowing it would not be long before he steered his new company back to his old advertising agency.

On the day we celebrated my daughter Nic's tenth birthday, helping out at the local stables, something she did most weekends, she fell off the horse she was riding and broke her arm. Unbeknown to her we had purchased a 14.2 hands horse from a girl who had recently worked for me. Nic already had an 11.2-hand pony by the name of Fonz. He was bought for her to ride at gymkhanas. This was fine but as Nic grew taller, Fonz didn't. And now she had outgrown gymkhanas. So the new horse was purchased to replace Fonz. He was a truly handsome Chestnut by name of Flame. He was introduced to Nic on her birthday. But for her broken arm, now heavily plastered, she would have ridden him home. There and then. It was love at first sight. A love that grew with every passing year, although he never once did what she asked of him. At any of the small local shows where they were entered it wasn't long before people stayed behind just to watch Nic and Flame perform. Somehow, somewhere, Flame had learned to jump in stages. Almost backwards. Finishing his jump facing the way from whence he came, with Nic screaming at him. For the life of me I can't remember who or where it was, but some bloke in the audience shouted "Come on Action Replay!" Few if any called him Flame again.

I had insisted that if and when we bought the replacement for Fonz then the little chap would be moved on. By then we had both horses stabled. This meant taking Nic to the stables before school and again, in the evening. The costs were excessive. Pat was now a driving instructor, successfully running her own school. So it fell to me to ferry Nic to wherever there and back was. That's when I decided Fonz was on his way. Have you ever faced a stable full of weeping young maidens? All pleading for Fonz to remain. All confessing their undying love for him. How he would die of sadness if he had to go elsewhere. How it would break Nic's heart. Enough's enough. I repented. And at the same time decided to have the four-stable block built on the land at the back of the house. It was fortuitous that I did. When Nic was eighteen, a close friend of hers, also eighteen, became pregnant. She also had a horse but not the finances to keep it. She asked Nic if she could keep it in our fourth stable, supposedly until the child was born. Nic asked me. I agreed. Provided it went back from whence it came. It never did. They rarely do. So now we had three ponies/horses in residence at 33 Rignals Lane, Galleywood. A block of four stables. Two one-acre paddocks.

But best of all I had merged my business with Shape. Accepted their request to be managing director, to retain the limited company registration. No argument from me. No sir. My cup runneth over. It was just a fifteen-minute drive from home to the Ingatestone office. Perfect. I say this because Nic was a veterinary nurse at a Blackmore practice, less than thirty minutes from Galleywood where complete with Grandmother Sylvia, horses Flame and Fonz, dogs Emma, Anna and Cleo, we're located. One big, happy, loving family. With Nic working with animals day by day, I knew the family was destined to grow. But I hadn't anticipated it being quite so soon.

It was one of her rare days off. Nic took her grandmother exploring. None of us knew the area well. I don't think Nic knew it at all. Nor did Cleo, Sylvia's dog who went with them. They parked in a small wooded area and set off. Whilst Nic made mental notes of things that stood out, she forgot she had a memory like a sieve. When it came to be time to go there was one question she had to answer first. Go where? She knew the answer. Home. But where was home? That she could not remember. Nor the right direction in which to head for Galleywood. Saved by the bell, as they say in boxing. Neither she nor Sylvia saw or heard him coming. He approached them from behind. Asked them who they were and what they were doing on his land. His tone curt. His attitude slightly menacing. Nic immediately apologised, explained we had only recently moved to Galleywood and hardly knew the lie of the land. Set out to explore with her grandmother and here they were. Hopelessly lost. The stranger's attitude softened. Especially when Nic told him, as they walked, she was a nurse with the local Blackmore vets. They were his vets too. Now she could see why he was short with them when first they met. They had unknowingly invaded his duck farm at a time when too many of his birds were being poached. They were now standing close to the farm's entrance. They could also see the small woodlands where Nic had parked the car.

They were saying their goodbyes when Sylvia spotted two young white ducks. She drew Nic's attention to them. "Aren't they lovely?" she said. "I'd love two like that."

"They are eight weeks old. It won't be too long before they are sold for the table," said the farmer. Nic bridled when she heard this and asked if she could buy them. Between her and her grandmother they could raise four pounds, thirty-five pence. To their surprise and delight it was accepted. They drove home very carefully, the young ducks in the boot. Just two more residents for us. It cost me £450 pounds to have a small pond and run erected. For reasons never revealed, they bit the hand that fed them. Mine. Whenever I appeared in the vicinity of their domain, they viciously attacked me. Being two males, were they punishing me for not providing them with female company? I never did find out. But being a red-blooded male, complete with red-blooded male desires, years later I still believe I was right.

TWELVE

The new Shape was developing satisfactorily. If only Grace hadn't died. There had been times when, on Friday shut-down, we sat in the pub before going home. The respect we had for each other was ever present. We often discussed life after Beacon. Both determined it could happen. She shared my belief that the new company should seek business in Europe. Assist comparable European companies to seek and find success in the UK. Then to do the same for Shape. Little did I know then it was already happening, thanks to Otto Prill in Holland. He was a bear of a man. Larger than life. As well as being founder of a small, award-winning Netherlands advertising agency, Otto was also one of Holland's foremost, recognised accomplished master chefs. A strange combination, but one that sat comfortably on his broad shoulders. We met through both of us working for the same UK client.

Jim Bishop was the client's publicity manager. Also, a keen golfer. We'd arranged a game. As ever my game was a mix of the good, the bad and the downright ugly. Over a pint in the club house, he mentioned Otto. He would be in the UK next week. Jim said I should meet him. He shared my interest in developing a network of like-minded, size-minded European Agencies. The difference being Otto had already set his European wheels in motion. He explained over lunch how he was in working relationships with agencies in Sweden and Belgium and had been for over two years. Early difficulties were minor. Swiftly eradicated. Now business between Otto and both countries ran smoothly and trouble-free. I liked what I heard. True to his word, from this meeting with Otto, I now knew of agencies in three countries able and willing to work with Shape in times of need. The idea of an established European network of European advertising agencies, ready, willing and able to provide the services needed, at prices clients were prepared to pay – my enthusiasm for this man's vision knew no bounds.

Within the year E3 was up and running. There for all to see and use if and when needed. So why E3? We all wanted Euro as the group's collective prefix. Sadly, extensive searching was rewarded with disappointment. Every possible usage of Euro had been registered long, long ago. So the compromise we settled on was E3. The established major road network running throughout Europe and recognised by every European. At the beginning there were just four agencies alerted to the distinct possibilities of becoming members of E3. Otto was my link with them. They in turn had working links with agencies or clients in other countries. All were alerted to E3. Interest gauged. Would they be willing to attend an inaugural meeting in Holland? All but two attended and E3 was born. It was a network of nine agencies. They were from Holland, UK, France, Switzerland, Germany, Belgium, Sweden, Finland and Denmark. I explained to Shape why we should be a founder member. There was total agreement. They were pleased when I told them all yearly AGMs would be conducted in English. I was particularly pleased when it was further agreed each AGM would be held in member countries.

Almost at once business opportunities emerged amongst E3 members. All members agreed the network needed leadership. Two candidates emerged. Otto Prill and Ed Bouchard of the Swiss-based Bouchard Agencies. Otto declined. Ed accepted. In a very short space of time he proved ideal as team leader. The man with all the right credentials. Through Shape's biggest client, I discovered there was a similar, though much bigger, American network of small to medium-sized agencies. Through Ed, I suggested we invite them to become our guest members. They accepted. They asked that we make a presentation of our credentials at their AGM in San Antonio later in the year. We did. Based upon the theatrical *Alice Doesn't Live Here Anymore*, Ed and I collaborated in putting the presentation together and making the presentation together. They loved it. Became lifetime members.

After three days of exceptional hospitality, we left for New York where we both had client meetings. The most memorable, enjoyable and successful week of my business life. With Shape coasting comfortably, I was conscious that the mental promise made when I joined was moving ever closer. We needed new premises. Modern offices that complemented eighteen months of confident business development, made ever more urgent when, during a rare, unusual heavy storm, our ground floor flooded. Jokingly I wrote a small piece for our trade and local press headed 'When the Business came Flooding in'. It resulted in a phone call from an insurance company managing director. He had earmarked a newly built two-storey building nearing completion in Brentwood. He was looking for tenants to occupy the ground floor. They would be ready to move into in three months. We took one look, argued and won a small decrease in rent, and were happily tenants within the three months. Loved the underground parking and had suitable room for expansion. Just about everything in my garden was bloody marvellous.

THIRTEEN

Since time immemorial, fathers with sons have paid homage to football. The beautiful game. So when Chris, my youngest son came home from his Cub meeting in tears, I wanted to know why. He told me. The manager of their football team was giving up at the end of the season. He was dreadfully upset. There was to be no more football. Unless one of the dads would take over as team manager. I sat him down and asked how many Cubs were there. Together, we counted twenty. I said surely one of their dads would replace him; if not, then I would until a new manager could be found. From what I could gather afterwards, within minutes of arriving at the next Cub meeting, God bless him, Satchel Mouth announced to all and sundry, "My dad said he'd love to be our new manager."

Later that evening, Terry, the Cub pack leader telephoned. He thanked me profusely and asked me would it be convenient to drop the kit, footballs *et al.* off at the weekend. Little did I believe at the time just how much enjoyment Cubs' football could be, especially what followed in the coming years. I became a boys' football club manager, did the course and qualified as a referee, only to officially retire at the age of seventy-two. The following Saturday morning I went to the next home game. We were slaughtered. At twenty-one to one I gave up counting. The visiting side were bigger, taller and far and away superior to us. The then-retiring manager explained you could play Cub football until you went on to be Scouts. Hence the difference. Most of his visiting team would be Scouts next season. Not one of the team I was about to inherit would be for the next few seasons at least. Immediately I could see the advantages to be gained in the seasons ahead.

Especially as nearly all my players went to Langton School. There and then I named them Langton Royals. They became one of the most successful teams over the next five years. I spoke to all of the team's parents and told them I was happy to be the Cub team manager for as long as they were Cubs and to continue on into league football, but only if the boys and parents wished to do so. Happily, both agreed. Hand on heart, I was heading into the most enjoyable and fulfilling years of my life. Apart from playing on Saturday mornings on the school pitch – with the head teacher's agreement – I had them training on Tuesday evenings. As expected, they won nothing for the rest of the season. But they started to shape up and stopped losing by huge scores. Began playing team football. Began to believe in themselves. Peter Webber, father of Steven, volunteered to work alongside me as co-manager. We called a parent meeting. Most turned up – it was in a pub! We told them of our plans. Like any football club, we needed funds. Peter and I outlined how we saw the future, both as members of a local league and socially. Would they support us in organising a dinner dance later in the year? We told them we were hoping that we could find a willing audience of 180–200. We sold 400 tickets. Langton Royals Football and Social Club was up and running.

In the next two years the boys improved massively. They dominated Cubs' football, winning the league and cup double. When the players were eleven, we were able to enter the Belhouse League. We learned a great deal in our first year, finishing fourth in a twelve-team under eleven league. All but one of the Langton school stayed together. The league rules demanded no matter what age group, every team must have seventeen registered players. The boys, when told we needed to sign five more players, duly obliged. Four new boys were quickly found. From that moment on, everything fell into place. Apart from watching a very talented football team at weekends we also planned to build a social team, organising an exciting programme of events, supported 100 per cent by our parents. In six years, we never finished out of the top three. We won the league and cup double three times. Topped the league table four times. Toured Wales at Easter; France and Spain the following season, winning all European games bar one. Had two boys playing for Essex.

It was Peter who suggested we toured Spain. The boys loved the idea so Peter went ahead and contacted a travel company who did overseas sporting tours. He prised an affordable two-night/three-day tour from them. Forty-four adults and sixteen boys were Spain-bound in early September. The flight was uneventful, although the aircraft which landed just after us could hardly say the same. It was Scottish. Half the passengers were carrying the other half off the plane. I think they must have boarded in Glasgow well-oiled and continued drinking once on board. They were a football team. From the state of them, I doubt they were able to field a sober full squad. Our players looked on in disbelief. Our hotel was rather old fashioned but comfortable.

It was Friday afternoon when we arrived. Our first game was Saturday afternoon. Plenty of time to get acquainted with our surroundings and get to know the hotel staff. The boys most certainly did. By evening they were on first-name terms. After dinner we relaxed. Come morning we went through a light training programme in preparation for the game. Kick-off was at three o'clock. We played well. Every boy got a game. We won comfortably 5–1. At full time their manager had laid on an enjoyable afternoon tea, prompting him to comment that "Langton Royals ate as well as they played." The parents were also well pleased with the team's performance. The hotel staff applauded them as they entered. Peter Webber and I told them how well they had played but warned they would need to lift their game tomorrow, telling them for the first time the team they were playing was a year older. It didn't seem to worry them one little bit. Sadly, they lost the game, against a side they were well capable of beating. A game they should have won.

After dinner I told them that the parents, Peter and I were going out for the evening. I told them we were going to a bar not far away. They would be expected to be on their best behaviour. Definitely no boozing. In bed and lights out at ten o'clock. To a boy they promised to behave. Being Saturday night, the bar was full. The music good and loud. Relaxed without the boys, perhaps we drank more than we should. Danced more than we should. Sang more than we should. This was the Brits, letting their hair down. At times we were mightily close to providing the cabaret. It was one hell of a terrific evening, loved by one and all. We arrived back at the hotel a little after 2am. It was in total darkness. As silent as a tomb. I went up to the first floor where the boys were room-sharing. Not a sound. Not a light left on. Silently I blessed them. Little did I know.

Peter and I were up early. Getting the kit, balls and first-aid kits together. We were in the middle of breakfast when the first of the boys appeared. Was it my imagination? Or did they sit as far away from Peter and I as they possibly could? Nor did they all appear for breakfast. There was something not right. Already I had a sinking feeling in the pit of my stomach. Normally when we travelled to far-away games by coach there was a constant buzz of conversation. Loud peals of laughter. Rude songs and rhymes. This was missing as we travelled to the opponents' ground. There was no nonstop chatter in the dressing room. When I asked did they disobey me, visit the bar and buy drinks, get the waiters to bring drinks up to them, no matter the boy who answered it was no to each question.

The handshakes. Handing over of club emblems. Referee introduction over. The whistle blew. The game was on. Although the age difference was supposed to be one year, their striker had a face full of stubble. Almost without exception, man for man they looked to be half a stone heavier. I won't dwell on the game, which we lost 3–2, but a few minutes in Steve Webber, who plays for Essex, our centre half, went for a high ball. He jumped high enough to have won it. Then in the very last instant, he withdrew his head from the path of the ball. The bugger had a hangover!!. Now I knew. I usually went into the dressing room with them at half-time. I sent Peter instead. He told them how disappointed and angry I was. What it cost to put this short tour together. That I was now considering leaving as manager. They came out. Started with all guns blazing. Apologised by scoring twice. Had one perfectly good goal disallowed for an offside that wasn't, restoring my belief in Langton Royals F.C. They were fourteen years old. So how did they get hold of the beer? I didn't know it, but behind the bar was an ancient dumb waiter. The boys sent their money down. The waiter sent the beer up. They told the truth. Not a boy visited the bar. Not a waiter visited the first floor. It was then I decided to take the course that would qualify me as a referee.

FOURTEEN

Having two Children. Both male. I'd decided long ago, that was enough. What I didn't know was after lengthy deliberation. Pat decided she wanted a daughter. Wish granted, there would be seven years between Christopher, my youngest son and new daughter. It was 1967. We were breakfasting. I'd had no pre warning of what was to come She simply said, pouring her second cup of tea, "Frank, if you refuse to help me create another balloon over the toyshop, the shutters are coming down. For good. Or until you change your mind." I was in shock. Not only by her demand. More so by how it was couched. Remnants of a joke she had heard many moons past. She later admitted it was her defence against future male dominance. When she told, Mike Watts, our family GP, he agreed on medical grounds. Best now rather than leave it later. We were lucky. She conceived almost immediately.

Mike Watts was our first and most personable family Doctor. He was small and rotund. Great with children. But then he should be. When he re-married, he'd added his children to his second wife's brood. He was now a ten children Dad. His knowledge and cures for children's ailments was legendary. He had a great sense of humour. A fund of medical tales from his time as a Hospital Surgeon. A keen lover of all sport. Especially Football. Fiercely loyal to his patients. Has this man no faults you may well ask. Yes he has. One. Unforgiveable to a Charlton Athletic supporter, which I am. For his sins he supports Arsenal Football Club.

Pat's pregnancy was troubled by high blood pressure. Mike regularly called at the house. If he hadn't she would have been hospitalised. During one of his visits. She told him she was going to insist I had a Vasectomy. He asked that I went to the Surgery to discuss where it should be done. I did. What he had to tell me was hard to believe. He was a qualified surgeon. However, as his family grew he found the cost of living seriously unaffordable. Then he discovered how much GPs could earn. Depending upon patient numbers. So he did what was necessary. The rest is history. "So Frank, I'll do the snip for you. Right here whenever you decide a date that's convenient." "That is of course if it's what you both want" As soon as I got home, I told Pat. It was then she told me she already knew. There and then the snip it was. Decision confirmed when I read a national press article by Michael Parkinson. He was one of the early "snip" volunteers. He said, "As they drew my private parts through the whole in the rubber sheet. It looked like a Frankfurter on a green salad."

The girl we both wanted duly arrived. Should ever I remarry a lady keen to have children, I was well and truly snookered. My weaponry was only able to fire blanks. A thought residing permanently in my anxious mind. Whenever and wherever I saw Mike. His short, rotund chubby body was encased in the longest red and white scarf you ever did see. He was never without it. Wrapped generously round his neck. With yards of it. Dancing jerkily alongside his body. When and wherever he walked. It told all and sundry they were in the presence of rabid Arsenal supporter. Setting another question that needed to be asked. Would a Charlton Athletic fan since birth, knowingly allow the sworn enemy within grappling distance of his manhood? Both were swiftly answered by Pat with a resounding YES ! Followed by a statement no regular "upforit" male bedroom warrior ever wished to hear. "No more bedroom frolics till it's done." On hearing that I immediately rang Mike. Asking him to bring the agreed date of the butchery. Forward by a month to the coming weekend."

So here I was. Naked from the navel down. Lying on a made up Surgery bed. Shaking with fear and trepidation. Mike now appearing. Slowly approaching. Holding what looked like garden shears. Red and white scarf. Trailing away into the distance.He spoke. A noticeable hint of merriment in his voice. " Do you know Frank. It's been a bloody long year since I last did this. Hope it all falls into place " I was speechless. Shut my eyes. Tight closed. It seemed an eternity. It was in fact seconds before Mike spoke. "Would you look at this. It all came back once I'd started. What do you think?" Mike was holding a short piece of what looked like plastic tubing. He asked would I like it for a keep sake. I said thanks but no thanks. I wanted nothing that reminded me I was no longer a complete man. A small piece of my anatomy which, gone in one fell swoop, rendered me a Eunuch.

I was ready to leave when Pat called to collect me, Mike began to dress my wounded pride.When finished, he stuffed the lot into what looked like a plastic hair net. I told him it was too tight.He said once I started to walk it would loosen. Also, he had another patient to go and see and needed to leave now. He left me sitting uncomfortably on his front garden wall and waved me goodbye. It was eleven o'clock and Pat was picking me up at eleven fifteen. I should have realised. No qualified Surgeon would ever have been asked to dress his performed surgery. The pick up time came. And went. Pat didn't. By a quarter to twelve I knew she had forgotten. I just had to go. I didn't know what hurt the most. My bum from sitting on a brick wall. Or my tightly strapped and netted cobblers. I faced a three quarter mile walk to my home. Most of it down hill. I stood and took my first step. A throbbing pain shot from my medically packaged, bruised and battered genitalia. By step three I knew I could go no further. What could I do. The only other way I could walk the long hill home was…backwards. And stooped. If anybody reading this remembers seeing a strange, limping, bent backward bloke crying through his tears. Yes folks. The answer to the mystery was me.

FIFTEEN

John Baker was managing director of a freight forwarding company. He was also a client of Shape, recently won by me. I was standing in his company reception, indulging my habit of arriving early for appointments, looking at a collection of photographs adorning the walls. Music. My constant companion since boyhood. Singing quietly to myself, suddenly a male voice interrupted my reverie.

"You've a nice voice Frank. Fancy joining a choir?" It was John, quietly arriving unseen. He'd stood listening for a short time before he spoke.

"I'd love to John, but I've never thought I was good enough. Besides which I don't read music." We were in the lift on our way to John's office on the third floor. Once seated, the first thing John explained was he could not read music either. He'd been a chorister for many years. Loved every minute and was looking forward to many years more. He sang with the South Woodham Ferrers Male Voice Choir. He said there were fifty-eight of them, and they were about to begin a three-month recruitment drive hoping to build the membership to seventy-five before touring Wales. Then jokingly John said if I didn't join he would look for another agency.

When I got home that evening, I told Pat about my meeting with John and his invitation for the two of us to attend the next choir rehearsal. We did. It was with her blessing I became a chorister. I was in my early fifties. On first glance though, the majority of my new choir looked the same. They didn't just sing *H.M.S. Pinafore*, most looked old enough to have crewed her maiden voyage. As a four-part male voice choir, I was welded onto the thirty-two other baritones. From the beginning, I learned to mime. Necessary until you were word perfect with all of the 103 numbers in our repertoire. For as far as I can remember, we never appeared on stage with a single sheet of music. That was taboo. When I joined, I was taught the art of mime. My mouth working in unison with the choir. It was the blokes singing either side of me – only they knew whether I was singing or not.

Four-part harmonies, dynamics, crescendos and the like were unchartered territory. I was told off for singing the baritone four part, not the melody; jingling my loose change in my pocket; looking miserable when singing numbers I did not enjoy. But I stayed the course, which surprised me, and finally became a valued member of South Woodham Ferrers Male Voice Choir, staying with them for twelve years. Were they good? Just a few years earlier they toured Wales and actually won an Eisteddfod. There were twelve Welshmen in the choir. That should tell you how good we were. And they still are. I firmly believe it was an apprenticeship I was destined to serve, especially the 'afterglow' which usually followed concerts to the nearest pub. But only having been given pre-permission from the Guv'nor first. Our music director was Stephen Rumsey, music teacher of Brentwood School. Brilliant. An excellent teacher. Full of fun. A great sense of humour. Whether rehearsing or in concert, to every man he was the very best there was. Without exception. Every chorister was shattered when told he was leaving. He was replaced by Frederick Dyer, an expert organist but whose only choir experience so we were told, was with young children, and it showed. The choir became increasingly unhappy, spending far too much time practising musical scales for entry into examinations none of us wanted. Except of course our new music director. I believe they eventually passed, long after I had left, a music director I wasn't happy with able to drive me away. I'm afraid so. Again it was something he decided to do.

Without reference to the choir committee or the choir, with a substantial chunk of our money he commissioned someone unknown except to himself to compose a piece of music which we could not believe. Nor to my knowledge afford or sing. I'm told it cost

£700 and we never did sing it. I had left before the 'dirge' was finished. It was never performed. It supposedly told the story of King Canute, bidding the waves at Canewden to recede. Meaningless, tuneless, pointless pound-wasting nonsense. Never sung by the choir. It was Freddy's farewell. Looking back on my first decade as a choir member but for the Dyer interlude, I loved every minute of becoming a seasoned songster.

But then again, nowhere near so much as I did with Chelmsford Male Voice Choir whom I sang with until we moved away. The choir had about forty members when I joined. No matter how hard we tried we were lucky to have recruited four new members in a year. I soon became publicity officer and a committee member. We had an excellent monthly newsletter. Good to read and write for. I also helped Brian, our secretary, with booking concerts, both home and away. I'd been constantly endeavouring to recruit new members. Then I had an idea. I wrote five pages of choir 'chat', answering all the questions which puzzled me until I joined Woodham Ferrers. I stood with two members of the choir outside Chelmsford Station, handing out my five-page 'What a Choir is and Does'. I also conscripted all members to mail-drop 200 copies of the same document either side of their own house, together with an invitation. It said there would be an open evening for you to come and listen to a rehearsal alone or with your wife. You will be very welcome. Listen and question. Meet the gang. Join the gang. I promise, you will never regret it. I never have. To our utter disbelief that evening twenty-three new choristers joined Chelmsford Male Voice Choir. They were still there years later when moving house forced me to leave.

My choir colleagues voted me a (singing) Gentleman and Scholar. Although it had been many years since I accepted the invitation to revamp Shape, I never lost contact with the top echelons of McLean Hunter management. When Ron Barnes died unexpectedly, the Canadians surprisingly appointed Robin Cobb, Publishing Editor of *Ports and Terminals*, as managing director. This being decades long gone, I cannot for the life of me remember what ever happened to Theo van Beek, but I do remember when Robin left to return to his first love, freelance journalism, this time my very good friend Gerald Brigg, Publisher of *British Printer*, was called upon to fill Robin's shoes. Knowing Gerald well, he said it was an excellent choice. Then promised one day to tell me where he'd buried van Beek's body (joke in poor taste). Eventually the Canadians sold the entire company but rewarded Gerald well for his stewardship. Never happy unless working, Gerald discovered a privately owned monthly magazine for the elderly, offered his services, promising to quadruple the advertising revenue by providing his years of selling experience, which I know was only second to one. Mine! After he said his goodbyes we decided the County of Essex was ready for its own business exhibition. We discussed the same with the Leader of Essex Council. He gave us his blessing after the Council gave him theirs. We contacted David Wilkins, who was building a growing exhibition company based in Potters Bar. We exchanged contracts and stand-selling began. Successfully. When the show ended, we decided it would remain a one-off, left to the professionals to take it on. No one ever did.

SIXTEEN

Though it took longer than at first targeted, Shape eventually reached a one million plus turnover. We had also added Debbie as our media buyer. She came from Saatchi and Saatchi, the biggest London-based advertising agency. She wasn't cheap but negotiated strong media advertising packages for Shape clients. This took the pressure off me, allowing me the time needed to create awareness of E3 in selected European agencies. A slow and time-consuming business. We had agreed to employ a second account executive. In the latter five years we took three on board. Each in turn seemed to be doing what was necessary. In each we invested the time they said would result in new accounts. It never did. Regretfully we had to say goodbye.

Over the years we had added substantial new UK business. Direct contact was made with the managing director of Countryside Properties. He allowed us to use new local press 'sell off the page' full- and half-page advertising campaigns. Up until then, new housing developments were publicised through estate agents. We decided to book large advertisements in local papers just where these developments were being built. The response surpassed our wildest expectations. Potential buyers were invited to visit the site; select the property they wanted; meet the Countryside sales team; purchase the property there and then. Deal done. End result, houses sold directly off the page. No estate agent fees. Client delighted. But we hadn't done our homework. In the next eighteen months we had added six new developers to our client list, all of them profitably established. They, like most builders, stopped building.

In the same period, we had recruited four new car dealerships. Now we faced the toughest UK recession ever. The bank rate had risen to 15 per cent. We had borrowed heavily when Shape began its advertising agency life. We needed an overdraft facility, which the bank granted, charging 4.5 per cent for the privilege. My co-directors ignored my warning that within two years we would need a financial brain on the payroll. They said no. Rely on what we had, a combination of Ian, June and an outside accountant. It wasn't enough. When E3 came along I took my eye off the ball. Of our current accounts, property developers and car dealerships, far and away presented the biggest combined area of business. Or should have done. But buyers of both decided they could stay where they were. Stay in the houses they had. Wait until the recession receded and mortgages were once again affordable and available. Drive the same car until the all-clear sounded. As I said earlier, the recession was not only financially cruel, it went on far too long. Especially for companies forced to rely on borrowed money. That was us.

I will never understand banks. The manager of our branch came from the Bournemouth branch where he had been happily settled. So the powers that be transferred him to Brentwood. Within a month his wife moved back to where she had been happily settled for years, leaving Stanley Beard to travel to Bournemouth every weekend. He was one of the old-style managers. Do something that made him unhappy, you were summoned to the bank. Sat down. Professionally castigated. Taken to the pub and bought a pint. We worked well together. I liked him a lot. A few months prior to the recession beginning he was transferred back to where we both knew he belonged. Back from whence he came. Why, he didn't know. His replacement was young enough to be my son. And nasty with it. He said he had been ordered to severely reduce the overdraft. This in the worst, costliest recession to date. Where the largest areas of our business activities had practically disappeared. We could not do what was ordered. We were immediately placed in receivership. A year later there was no more Shape. No more E3, which was indeed a great pity. You may well ask why, because I had

just won Shape the Commodore Computer Account.
Advertising budget £964,000. I stood in the dust where
my desk used to be and wept.

SEVENTEEN

I had time on my hands. No more European or American E3 trips. When I suggested representing their UK interests, they said no. That's when I put the idea of an Essex business exhibition to the Brentwood Council leader. He was immediately in favour. As was Gerald Brigg. Together he and I represented highly experienced sales potential with the advantage of exhibition stand buildings costed by David Wilkins. It was all systems go, after which I would retire. Which I did, concentrating on what had been happening on the home front. Had our Galleywood home stood in or near water, then it would have been a replica of Noah's Ark. Our love of animals, all animals, ran family deep. For example, in March this year after a celebratory sixty-second wedding anniversary dinner, I asked the question "Pat, How many dogs have we rescued altogether in our married life?" She answered by reeling off the names of each and every one. I was gobsmacked as she finished with Bonnie, our current Romanian inmate. Sandie, Sophie, Bella, Emma, Cilla, Kylie, Rubie, Cindy, Ruby, Christie, Amber, Cleo, Bonnie, Finn, Maddie, from different rescue sources. Maddie was delivered at 7.30am by the Romanian charity. Five days ago. As with most, she's timid, wary, alert to even the smallest sound. But her tail is slowly starting to wag. She is beginning to accept we are friend, not foe, to fifteen otherwise condemned innocents, each of them remaining with us for the rest of their natural lives. From 1982 to the present day, exchanging fear and dread for endless TLC and normality.

Pat grew up with a most kind, considerate and generous maiden aunt. Beryl by name, sister to Pat's mother. She was a Fellow of the Royal Zoological Society, a privilege of which was allowing her to visit London Zoo on Sunday mornings. Once there, being able to hold certain selected animals before the Zoo opened. She would sometimes take Pat with her. She loved taking advantage of holding the permitted animals, taking penguins for walks, feeding dog biscuits to giraffes in their enclosure. Now you know where her deep-seated love of animals was born, which affected every member of our family from early childhood.

Now we had Galleywood paddocks and stables, with my daughter working for a local vet, the animals came in two by two. Obviously, our dog family didn't all happen at the same time. However, we did have five, including Kylie, the Irish Wolfhound, at the house. And at the same time we also had little Fonz and Flame (Action Replay). Then unexpectedly along came Solitaire (Solly). So horses? Now there were three. Sue, Solly's previous owner, came visiting quite often, bringing her baby with her. Then a further surprise. Nic's eighty-four-year-old grandmother insisted on doing the morning muck-out. Nic also had a part-time Saturday job with a small but busy greengrocer. One of the regular customers discussed two lambs she was desperately trying to re-home. Almost before she had time to say their names, Daisy and Bear were winging their way to 33 Rignals Lane.

This was the early days of the stampede of the new-to-England pot-bellied Vietnamese pigs. Did I find them amusing? Yes! But had no desire to have them on the premises. Other people thought differently, deciding to breed them to meet the growing demand of people wanting them for pets. I know not how it came about but the family who bred them on their council property were told "get rid or get out" and I was told there were six infants needing new homes. Would you believe it, Nic was the first to hold up her hand. Became mum to Brazen and Bashful. They came from the same mother yet one was shy and retiring, the other aggressive and in your face. Their names, chosen by me, suited ideally.

You will remember earlier in the book how two white young ducks became our first tenants and how I needed to have a small pond and shelter constructed. Both were male and without a lady they became vicious. Attacked me whenever the opportunity arose. The pigs needed similar accommodation but much larger and without the pond. Both needed to be fox-proof. And they were. Our five dogs were very well behaved but never allowed in the paddocks unless accompanied by an adult. Mark you, if ever an adult, male or female, found their way there alone they would be foolish to take Brazen head-on. What's more, I could never understand intelligent people having them as indoor pets. But they did. And I am told, indoors they were remarkably clean.

EIGHTEEN

So there they are. Memoirs of Frank William Payne. Born on the same day as Her Majesty The Queen, April 21st, 1934. Aged eighty-seven next year. Desperate to become 100 not out. If and when I do, I will send Her Majesty a telegram congratulating her on being the longest-serving and best loved monarch this country has ever been blessed with. You've got to admit it's different. I sincerely hope you have enjoyed reading Memoirs 1 and 2 as much as I have writing them. Life has been kind. My family masterful. Cancer came calling thrice. As neither was invited, all were sent packing with their backsides in slings. I doubt either has the temerity to call again. Nor do I feel existing circumstances will give me time enough to start and finish Memoirs 3. I am however contemplating writing a series of short stories. If I do, you will be the first to know. In the mean time, the money raised by both Memoirs 1 and 2 is for SeSaw, a small, local, Suffolk animal rescue centre. They do a sterling job with limited resources. Their needs are therefore far greater than mine.

As I said earlier in Memoirs 2, if either you, a family member, a relative or friend are contemplating homing a rescued dog, hesitate no longer. They will repay you with love and loyalty by the ton. Every minute of every waking hour. As I write this, Maddie, one of a batch of fifteen dogs rescued in Romania, was brought to England. She has been brutalised, as many Romanian street dogs are. Watching her bonding with my daughter and granddaughters is wonderful to behold. I doubt she has received one act of kindness in the eighteen months she has lived. That is until Saving Romanian Strays found her, brought her back to England and delivered her to us. She is gradually accepting TLC is par for the course here and already she has started to return it. With interest. She is our second Romanian rescued dog; Bonnie was our first. She came to us five years ago. Long forgotten is the terror with which her life began. She has been the perfect companion for Pat and I ever since. So please, if you are thinking of having a dog, have a rescued dog. I promise you will have canine love, gratitude and loyalty for life.

As I bid my farewell, I share with you something that will put a smile on the face of dog-lovers the world over:

The Dog

Once God had made the Earth and sky
The flowers and the trees
He then made all the animals
All the birds and the bees
When his work was finished
Not one was quite the same
"Now I'll walk this earth of mine
And give each one a name."
So he travelled land and sea
And everywhere he went
A little creature followed him
Until its strength was spent
When all were named upon the Earth
As well as sky and sea
The little creature said "Dear Lord
There's not one left for me."
God stopped and smiled then softly said,
"I've left you to the end,
"My own name I've turned back to front
And called you Dog, my friend."

Anon.